SCHOLASTIC

Fluency
LESSONS
for the Overhead

GRADES
4–6

by Alyse Sweeney

NEW YORK • TORONTO • LONDON • AUCKLAND • SYDNEY

MEXICO CITY • NEW DELHI • HONG KONG • BUENOS AIRES

Teaching *Resources*

For David

Excerpt from *Giving Thanks: The 1621 Harvest Feast* by Kate Waters. Copyright © 2001 by Kate Waters. Reprinted by permission of Scholastic Inc.

"Shadows" by Anna Hutt from *Kids' Poems: Teaching Third & Fourth Graders to Love Writing Poetry* by Regie Routman. Copyright © 2000 by Regie Routman. Reprinted by permission of Scholastic Inc.

"Spider" from *Animals Nobody Loves* by Seymour Simon. Copyright © 2001 by Seymour Simon. Reprinted by permission of Chronicle Books.

Excerpt from *Clem's Chances* by Sonia Levitin. Copyright © 2001 by Sonia Levitin. Reprinted by permission of Scholastic Inc.

"My Mother Says I'm Sickening" by Jack Prelutsky from *The New Kid on the Block* by Jack Prelutsky. Copyright © 1984 by Jack Prelutsky. Reprinted by permission of HarperCollins.

Excerpt from *The British Are Coming!* by C. White. Copyright © by Scholastic Inc. Reprinted by permission of Scholastic Inc.

"My Dad" by Sherri Tysinger from *Kids' Poems: Teaching Third & Fourth Graders to Love Writing Poetry* by Regie Routman. Copyright © 2000 by Regie Routman. Reprinted by permission of Scholastic Inc.

Excerpt from *The Music of the Dolphins* by Karen Hesse. Copyright © 1996 by Karen Hesse. Reprinted by permission of Scholastic Inc.

"Armed Attack" from *Flies Taste With Their Feet: Weird Facts About Insects* by Melvin and Gilda Berger. Copyright © 1997 by Melvin and Gilda Berger. Reprinted by permission of Scholastic Inc.

Excerpt from *Harry Potter and the Sorcerer's Stone* by J. K. Rowling. Copyright © 1997 by J. K. Rowling. Reprinted by permission of Christopher Little Literary Agency.

Excerpt from *P.S. Longer Letter Later* by Paula Danziger and Ann M. Martin. Copyright © 1998 by Paula Danziger and Ann M. Martin. Reprinted by permission of Scholastic Inc.

"The Turtle" by Arnold Spilka from *Monkeys Write Terrible Letters* by Arnold Spilka. Copyright © 1994 by Arnold Spilka. Reprinted by permission of Arnold Spilka.

Excerpt from *Kater Kids* by Anne Miranda. Copyright © 2002 by Scholastic. Reprinted by permission of Scholastic Inc.

"Talking to the Horse Trainer" by Nancy Springer from *Music of Their Hooves* by Nancy Springer. Copyright © 1994 by Nancy Springer. Reprinted by permission of Woodsong/Boyds Mill Press.

"Untitled Chant" from *Writing Funny Bone Poems* by Paul Janeczko. Copyright © 2001 by Paul Janeczko. Reprinted by permission of Scholastic Inc.

Cover design by Maria Lilja
Interior design by Sydney Wright

Product ISBN: 0-439-58853-7
Book ISBN: 0-439-58858-8
Copyright © 2004 by Alyse Sweeney
Published by Scholastic Inc.
All rights reserved. Printed in the U.S.A.

3 4 5 6 7 8 9 10   40   13 12 11 10 09 08 07 06 05

Contents

Introduction

Direct and explicit. As with all areas of reading instruction, direct and explicit is the name of the game when it comes to fluency instruction. When you model for students how text should sound when read aloud, you help them enormously. But when you talk about *why* you emphasize particular words or phrases, read at varying speeds, and clump certain words together, students learn that meaning is carried not only by the words, but by the way the reader interprets and expresses the words.

What Is Fluency?

Fluency is the ability to read text accurately and effortlessly at an appropriate rate and with meaningful phrasing and intonation. Students who lack fluency read in a choppy, word-by-word manner. This lack of fluency is directly related to poor comprehension (Nathan and Stanovich, 1991). Some students who lack fluency spend most of their energy decoding words, leaving them with little energy for comprehending. Readers must have automatic recognition of words in order to read them in context and relate them to background knowledge so comprehension can take place (Snow, Burns, Griffin, 1998). Other students read words accurately, but their poor phrasing and intonation hampers their comprehension; it is often the phrases, versus individual words, that hold meaning (Rasinski, 2003).

Maryanne Wolf and Tami Katzir-Cohen (2001) have further defined fluency as a developmental process that involves all the components of reading acquisition, including phonemic awareness and decoding skills, as well as a strong vocabulary, knowledge of grammatical functions, and knowledge of word roots and parts. This definition moves away from the notion that fluency is an outcome that can be improved upon once the child already knows how to read. Rather, it supports the idea of making explicit fluency instruction a part of reading instruction from the very beginning. Wolf and Katzier-Cohen advocate teaching fluency at the letter pattern and word level. For instance, we can teach students to recognize chunks automatically (for example, *-an*) and have them practice reading word family words quickly (*can, man, pan*, etc.).

Fluency Instruction Makes Its Way Into Classrooms

Until recently, fluency instruction was largely ignored. In fact, Richard Allington (1983) described fluency as "the most neglected" skill in reading. Today, fluency is viewed as a critical component of reading instruction and of a child's reading development. The report of the National Reading Panel (2000) addresses the important role of fluency in reading instruction and many states and curriculum guidelines now include oral reading fluency as one of the many measures used in literacy assessment. A large-scale study by the National Assessment of Educational Progress (Pinnell et al., 1995) found that 44 percent of fourth graders did not have the level of fluency needed to comprehend on grade level.

> ### Fluency Terms
>
> **phrasing**—the way words are chunked together, marked by pauses
>
> **rate**—the speed at which we read
>
> **intonation**—the emphasis given to particular words or phrases

Building Fluency With Fluency Lessons for the Overhead: Grades 4–6

A Look at Each Lesson

Fluency Lessons for the Overhead: Grades 4–6 is a collection of 15 lessons. Each lesson has these elements: a student page with a carefully selected reading passage and a "Fun With Fluency" activity; an overhead transparency with the reading passage on it; and a teacher page, with a four-part instructional guide that incorporates best practices in fluency instruction. The instruction is organized into the following four components:

* a focus on comprehension ("Meaning First" component that focuses attention on the author's intended meaning; this focus continues through the "Model and Discuss Fluency" component)
* modeling ("Model and Discuss Fluency" component)
* guided practice ("All Together Now" component)
* independent practice ("Practice, Practice, Practice!" component)

The reading passages include poems and excerpts from both popular fiction and nonfiction. These passages are provided in two formats—as both transparencies and as blackline student reproducibles. The varied formats offer you several options for instructional presentation. For instance, the transparencies can serve as a powerful tool for modeling fluency because students can easily view the text as you read it aloud and point out the features that give clues to how to read. The transparencies are also a time-saver, allowing you to spend more time on instruction, and less time on lesson preparation. The reproducibles include a copy of the reading passages, which provides each student with opportunities for independent reading practice. In addition, the reproducibles provide a "Fun With Fluency" activity that reinforces fluency concepts presented in the lesson and extends students' comprehension of the passage.

Lesson Walk-Through To help you better envision the elements of each lesson and its intended use, see the diagrammatic "walk-through" lesson on pages 6 and 7.

The fluency spotlight highlights the fluency element(s) that are the focus of the lesson. Feel free to draw students' attention to other fluency elements as you see fit.

Each fluency lesson begins with a Read Aloud and discussion of the passage. Use the discussion questions provided, or create your own, to help students focus on the meaning of the passage before exploring the fluency topics.

The lesson proceeds to a script that serves as a guide for a modeled reading of the passage. Here, invite students to listen carefully to *how* you read the text—ideally from the transparency of the passage so that students can easily follow along as you point to and discuss the text. The goal is to keep the instruction direct and explicit as you explain *why* you read the text the way you do.

This section provides an assisted reading activity, in which students take part in the reading. The variety of echo and choral reading activities help students attain fluency with the passage alongside a fluent reader— the teacher, other adult, or even a fluent student. Again, the transparency is an effective tool for helping students follow along and make the connection between how written words and special text features look and the way the words sound when read aloud. The assisted reading activities can take place multiple times over the days following the modeled reading for reinforcement and practice.

The variety of activities in this section provide opportunities for students to practice reading the passage, either independently or with partners. Several activities culminate in a reading performance. As with the assisted reading activities, these activities can be repeated as necessary for reinforcement.

Reading Passage D: Excerpt from *Clem's Chances*

FLUENCY SPOTLIGHT

Commas

PART 2
The Power of Punctuation

MEANING FIRST

Before the modeled reading, read aloud and discuss the passage. Pose these or other comprehension questions: *Where and when might this story take place? What are the clues in the text that led you to your answer?* Talk about the vocabulary in the text (*dread, courted, prospects, doused*). Now continue with the lesson and read the text again with a focus on fluency.

MODEL AND DISCUSS FLUENCY

Proceed with a modeled reading of the excerpt from *Clem's Chances*, stressing the pause at each comma. Use the script provided here as a sample for your own instructional dialogue with students.

"Commas signal the reader to take a brief pause. Sometimes commas separate a list of items, characteristics, or events, such as in this sentence: **All in a single day I'd courted death, seen disaster, heard of massacres.** *Did you hear the way I paused slightly after each event? Now look at the commas in the next sentence and listen as I pause at each:* **I had a fleeting thought of turning back, but where could I go, friendless and poor and without prospects?** *Listen as I read this sentence again without the commas. (Read it without pauses.) The sentence sounds choppy and unnatural—not at all like I would say it if I were speaking. The last sentence is a super-long sentence, with a whopping five commas to separate each idea. The commas are really needed here to help with the flow of the sentence:* **I must have slept, for the next thing I knew, there was Hank standing over me, and I lay in a puddle of water, for a sudden rain had doused me, and even my socks were soaking wet.** *The pauses also slow me down so I can visualize the many events and details in the sentence."*

ALL TOGETHER NOW

Do a line-by-line echo reading of the text, stressing the commas. Point to each word on the transparency as the students follow along. After several readings, invite volunteers to read a sentence to the class in a fluent manner.

Practice, Practice, Practice!

Partner Reading: Have partners take turns reading the excerpt from *Clem's Chances*. For partners of the same ability, have one student read the passage three times to a partner and receive feedback. Then have the partners switch roles. For partners of different abilities, pair above-level readers with on-level readers and on-level readers with below-level readers. The fluent reader can be a peer or an older student. First, the stronger reader models fluent reading with a paragraph or the entire passage. As the less fluent reader reads the same text aloud, the fluent reader provides assistance when needed, as well as feedback and encouragement. The less fluent reader rereads the text until it is read accurately and with fluency.

23

Name: _____   **Date:** _____

Excerpt from **Clem's Chances**
(by Sonia Levitin)

My companions were soon worn out from the talk. I began to hear their snores. But I sat up half the night, shivering, haunted by feelings of dread. My journey had just begun. All in a single day I'd courted death, seen disaster, heard massacres. I had a fleeting thought of turning back, but where could I go, friendless and poor and without prospects?

I must have slept, for the next thing I knew, there was Hank standing over me, and I lay in a puddle of water, for a sudden rain had doused me, and even my socks were soaking wet.

Fun With Fluency

1. Write your own sentence in which commas are used to separate a series of items, characteristics, or events, like in this sentence from the text: *All in a single day I'd courted death, seen disaster, heard massacres.*

_____

_____

_____

2. Write your own sentence in which commas are used to join two independent clauses, like in this sentence from the text: *I had a fleeting thought of turning back, but where could I go, friendless and poor and without prospects?*

_____

_____

_____

Fluency Lessons for the Overhead: Grades 4–6 Scholastic Teaching Resources, page 24

An Overview of the Book

Part 1: Phrasing, Rate, and Intonation In Part 1 of this book, students learn the three components of reading fluency: phrasing, rate, and intonation. They learn to think about what they read and have the author's intended meaning guide them to clump words together, emphasize certain words, and determine how quickly or slowly to read the text. Students also learn that the more they practice reading aloud a text, the smoother and more natural the words sound.

Part 2: The Power of Punctuation In Part 2, students learn that punctuation marks serve as signals. Each of the four poems highlights a particular punctuation mark that indicates to readers when to pause, when to emphasize words and read with emotion, when to raise their voice to indicate a question, or when to speak in another character's voice. The goal of this section is to help students understand that punctuation communicates how the author wants us to read the text. Acknowledging punctuation in text also helps us read the words in a natural manner, as if we were speaking.

Part 3: Putting It All Together Part 3 includes eight reading passages and poems in which students encounter a variety of punctuation and typographical signals. Modeled reading of the texts demonstrates several moods, sentence structures, and rhythms. As you explore the passages, talk explicitly about clues in the text that indicate how the words should sound when read aloud. Review and hand out the Fluent Reading Checklist on page 32. Encourage students to refer to the list when they feel their oral reading lacks expression and fluency or when they want to be sure to accurately communicate the author's meaning.

Appendix: Phrased Text Lessons The three Phrased Text Lessons (PTL) found in the Appendix are designed for students who regularly read in a word-by-word manner. These students are not grouping words into meaningful phrases, and therefore, their comprehension is weak. The step-by-step Phrased Text Lesson outlined by Rasinski (2003) provides explicit instruction in chunking words into meaningful segments with actual cues, or slashes, that are incorporated in the text and signal the reader when to pause.

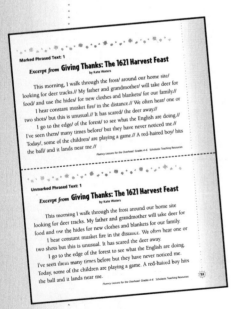

How Fluency Lessons for the Overhead: Grades 4–6
Reflects Best Instructional Practices

Rasinski (2003) has identified effective instructional methods for teaching fluency:

Model fluent reading. When you model fluent reading and explain *why* you emphasize particular words or phrases, read at varying speeds, and clump certain words together, students learn the importance of acknowledging typographical features and interpreting the author's words.

- *Fluency Lessons for the Overhead* includes a sample script ("Model and Discuss Fluency" component) that serves as a framework for modeling an aspect of fluency and discussing the given reading passage.

Provide oral support for readers. Fluency and comprehension improve when students simultaneously read and listen to a fluent rendition of the text. There are several forms of supported reading, including choral reading and echo reading.

- *Fluency Lessons for the Overhead* suggests a guided practice activity (the "All Together Now" activity) with each lesson.

Provide opportunities for independent practice. Like all skills, practice is essential for fluency. It is well documented that repeated reading leads to improved fluency. With each reading, the reader's focus shifts from the mechanics of decoding to interpreting the words and applying the appropriate phrasing and intonation.

- *Fluency Lessons for the Overhead* pairs each reading passage with a motivating oral reading activity and stresses independent practice ("Practice, Practice, Practice!" activity).

Focus instruction on meaningful phrasing. In addition to being able to decode quickly and effortlessly, fluent readers use pauses to break text into meaningful chunks. Meaning often lies in the phrases of a text, rather than in individual words.

- *Fluency Lessons for the Overhead* explicitly addresses phrasing throughout the book and provides three phrased text lessons (Appendix, page 51).

Provide text written at the reader's independent reading level. Independent level text is relatively easy for the reader, who reads with 95 percent success (no more than roughly 1 in 20 difficult words).

- *Fluency Lessons for the Overhead* includes poems, fiction, and nonfiction reading passages written at varying levels of difficulty to meet the needs of students.

In his foreword found in *The Fluent Reader* (Rasinski, 2003), James Hoffman encourages teachers to tightly incorporate comprehension into fluency instruction.

- *Fluency Lessons for the Overhead* begins each lesson with an oral reading that first and foremost addresses the meaning of the passage ("Meaning First"). Only then does the teacher dive into the fluency lesson. Additionally, the "Model and Discuss Fluency" section consistently addresses the author's intended meaning and the ways in which the author communicates this intended meaning.

Tips for Using *Fluency Lessons for the Overhead*

* The fluency lessons are appropriate for individual, small group, or whole class lessons.

* Ideally, the modeling, guided reading, and independent reading practice take place over several days, for about twenty to thirty minutes a day.

* The book is set up in three parts. Part 2 builds on information from Part 1, and Part 3 builds on information from Part 2. However, within each part, there is no recommended sequence to follow. You can select the passages based on the reading passage topic, genre, or the fluency focus listed at the top of each lesson.

* Each reading passage comes in the form of a transparency and student reproducible. It may be more manageable for students to read off the transparency while you model reading the passage and during the guided practice. Remember to run a pointer under the words as you read them so students can keep their place. Hand out the student reproducible page when students are ready for the independent reading activity in the "Practice, Practice, Practice!" section.

* Keep comprehension in the forefront of fluency instruction and share with students the goal of fluency instruction—to increase comprehension by reading smoothly, accurately, and with expression.

* Send the reproducible reading passages home with students so they can practice and read for family members.

"Fluency is a wonderful bridge to comprehension and to a lifelong love of reading."
                                                                            —Maryanne Wolf

PART 1

Phrasing, Rate, and Intonation
An Introduction

Effective fluency instruction, like all reading instruction, is direct and explicit. If the goal is for students to read with fluency, students need to understand and verbalize what a fluent reader does. Below are three mini-lessons that explain three components of fluency: proper phrasing, rate, and intonation. It is not important that students know these terms, only what they mean. The sample sentence below and the following three reading passages have little punctuation and typographical signals to demonstrate that our interpretation of the words and our knowledge of speech patterns guides us when we read.

Write the following sentence on the chalkboard or chart paper: Matt loves spaghetti and meatballs.

Phrasing is the way words are chunked together, marked by pauses.
First read the sentence in a word-by-word manner. Ask students how the sentence sounded. Explain that fluent readers chunk or group words together and use slight pauses between the clusters of words to make the reading sound more natural, like talking. Read the sentence with meaningful phrasing (*Matt loves / spaghetti and meatballs*). Talk about how some words sound natural *squished* together without a pause, like *spaghetti and meatballs, peanut butter and jelly* and *birthday cake*.

Rate is the speed at which we read.
Read the sentence slowly and monotone. Then read it at a natural speed. Do students hear the difference in the way the sentence was read? Which way did they like you to read it? Explain that fluent readers read at a speed similar to talking. The more they practice reading a particular text, the more natural and smooth they will sound. Let students know that the goal is not to read as quickly as possible, but to read at a natural speaking rate. Sometimes, however, the text makes more sense when read slowly or quickly. For example, *Hurry! Everybody hide or we'll ruin the surprise!* is best read quickly, while, *Slowly, the snail slithered down, down, down the window* is best read slowly.

Intonation is the emphasis given to particular words or phrases.
As you read the sentence, emphasize a different word each time, pointing to that word as you read.

     1. **Matt** loves spaghetti and meatballs.

     2. Matt **loves** spaghetti and meatballs.

     3. Matt loves spaghetti and **meatballs**.

Did students hear the difference in the way the sentence was read? Talk about how emphasizing different words changes the focus in the sentence. In version 1, we are meant to focus on the fact that it is Matt, and not someone else, who loves this dish. In version 2, we are meant to understand that Matt is really, really fond of spaghetti and meatballs. In version 3, we are meant to focus on the fact that it is spaghetti and meatballs, rather than spaghetti without meatballs that Matt finds delicious.

FLUENCY SPOTLIGHT

Phrasing, Rate, and Intonation

MEANING FIRST

Before the modeled reading, read aloud and discuss the passage. Pose this or another comprehension question: *What message about the harvest feast is the author trying to pass on to the reader?* Now continue with the lesson and read the text again with a focus on fluency.

MODEL AND DISCUSS FLUENCY

Proceed with a modeled reading of the excerpt from *Giving Thanks: The 1621 Harvest Feast*, reading naturally and with expression. Use the script provided here as a sample for your own instructional dialogue with students.

Phrasing: *"Reading with fluency sounds a lot like the way people speak. When we talk, we naturally smoosh certain words together, as opposed to reading / each / word / one / at / a / time / separated / by / a / pause (demonstrate choppy, word-by-word reading). Let's look at the first sentence. Watch as I draw a slash on the overhead after clumps of words that seem to go together. **This morning / I walk through the frost / around our homesite / looking for deer tracks.** Listen to the slight pauses I make and the way I clump together the words between the slashes as I read this sentence. Now let's erase my slash marks and make random slash marks in the sentence: **This / morning I walk through the / frost / around our / home site looking for deer / tracks.** Listen as I read the sentence. Very unnatural-sounding, right? So even though this sentence does not have any commas or other punctuation to tell you to pause, fluent readers still insert pauses and clump words together in natural places to make the reading sound a lot like how people speak."*

Rate: *"When you read aloud, how do you know how fast or slow to read? One way is to think about the meaning of the words you read. For example, if you are reading the play-by-play of an exciting basketball game, you might read quickly, the way a sports announcer speaks quickly to keep up with the action. In this passage, the narrator is describing events and changes that are taking place near his home site. I imagine that he would speak these words at a natural speed—not too fast and not too slow. However, while we don't have the rest of the text in front of us, I can imagine that as the English boy comes close to the narrator to retrieve his ball, the narrator might continue in a fast and nervous tone."*

Intonation: *"Listen as I read this sentence from the text and tell me which word I emphasized: **We often hear one or two shots but <u>this</u> is unusual.** I emphasized the word **this** because it draws attention to the fact that the situation he is describing is out of the ordinary. When I emphasize **this**, it is easier to hear the concern in the narrator's voice. Here is another way I can read the sentence and show the narrator's concern: **We often hear <u>one</u> or <u>two</u> shots but this is unusual.**"*

ALL TOGETHER NOW

Do a choral reading of the text, pointing to each word as you read. Emphasize the phrasing, particularly in the long sentences. Explain that this reading passage has very little punctuation to tell the reader which words to clump together, which words to emphasize, or how fast or slow to read. It is up to the reader to think about what they are reading and decide how it would sound the most natural.

Practice, Practice, Practice!

Partner Reading: Have partners take turns reading the passage. For partners of the same ability, have one student read the passage three times to a partner and receive feedback. Then have the partners switch roles. For partners of different abilities, pair above-level readers with on-level readers and on-level readers with below-level readers. The fluent reader can be a peer or an older student. First, the stronger reader models fluent reading with a paragraph or the entire passage. As the less fluent reader reads the same text aloud, the fluent reader provides assistance when needed, as well as feedback and encouragement. The less fluent reader rereads the text until it is read accurately and with fluency.

Name: _____   Date: _____

Excerpt from **Giving Thanks: The 1621 Harvest Feast**
by Kate Waters

This morning I walk through the frost around our home site looking for deer tracks. My father and grandmother will take deer for food and use the hides for new clothes and blankets for our family.

I hear constant musket fire in the distance. We often hear one or two shots but this is unusual. It has scared the deer away.

I go to the edge of the forest to see what the English are doing. I've seen them many times before but they have never noticed me. Today, some of the children are playing a game. A red-haired boy hits the ball and it lands near me.

Fun With Fluency

In a soft voice, read the sentences below. For each pair of sentences, underline the words in bold that sound natural when "squished" together.

Example:

I hear constant musket **fire in** the distance.
I hear constant <u>**musket fire**</u> in the distance.

1. We often hear **one or two** shots but this is unusual.
   We often hear one or two **shots but** this is unusual.

2. I've seen them many **times before but** they have never noticed me.
   I've seen them **many times before** but they have never noticed me.

3. A red-**haired boy** hits the ball and it lands near me.
   A red-haired boy hits the ball and it lands near me.

FLUENCY SPOTLIGHT

Phrasing, Rate, and Intonation

MEANING FIRST

Before the modeled reading, read aloud and discuss the poem. Pose these or other comprehension questions: *How does this poem make you feel? What are some things the poet does to create the scary and suspenseful mood of the poem?* Now continue with the lesson and read the poem again with a focus on fluency.

MODEL AND DISCUSS FLUENCY

Proceed with a modeled reading of "Shadows," reading slowly and with expression to communicate the fear and anxiety the narrator feels. Use the script provided here as a sample for your own instructional dialogue with students.

Phrasing: *"Sometimes authors and poets use a series of short sentences, followed by a long sentence, to add drama to the text or poem and make it sound more interesting. Look at the way this poet uses short phrases and even just one word on a line to add drama to this very powerful poem. And listen as I pause at the end of each line. The many pauses work to create the scary mood of the poem."*

Rate: *"When you read aloud, remember to think about the speed at which you think those words would be spoken. In 'Shadows' the poet describes something that is terrifying and dramatic. She uses short phrases to create a feeling of anxiety. I can imagine that if she were here reading this text to us, she might read these short sentences in a somewhat slow and deliberate way. If they are read too quickly, the poem will not be as scary because the reader may not have enough time to think about each scary image. When I pause for an extra moment before reading the next line, I hope to build suspense for the listener."*

Intonation: *"When we draw attention to certain words, we pay even more attention to their meaning. In this case, the poet clearly emphasizes certain words by repeating them:* **Shadows seeing / Seeing everything / Seeing that I am scared / Seeing that I hurry to get into the sunlight.** *Therefore, when I read the poem, I stress the word* **seeing**, *and it helps to unleash the natural rhythm in the poem."*

ALL TOGETHER NOW

Begin with a line-by-line echo reading of "Shadows." Read with clear phrasing and dramatic intonation, pointing to the words on the overhead as the class reads aloud. Note that in this poem it is not punctuation that dictates the dramatic pauses, but the way the poem is organized. Move into a choral reading of the text.

Practice, Practice, Practice!

Tape-Assisted Reading: Tape-assisted reading is a motivating way for students to build fluency. Begin by creating a tape of "Shadows." You may want to have other adults or fluent readers create the tape to give students a variety of voices to listen to. First, students listen to the passage on tape, pointing to the words on their hard copy as they follow along. The students then read aloud with the tape, as they would in choral reading. Provide a purpose for students to practice and perform by inviting them to make their own tape of the reading passage. Challenge them to see how close they can make their version of the reading sound like the original taped reader. Perhaps their version can replace the original and serve as the new model for that reading passage!

Name: _____   Date: _____

Shadows

(by Anna Hutt from *Kids' Poems: Teaching Third & Fourth Graders to Love Writing Poetry*)

Shadows
Shadows creeping
In my closet
Under my bed
Shadows watching . . .
Watching every move I make
Watching . . .
From behind the bookcase
And in the dusty dresser drawers
Shadows looking
Around the corner
Upon the stairway
Behind the rocking chair that creaks when it rocks
Shadows staring
Staring through me
From next to the sofa
And staring through the keyhole in the attic door
Shadows seeing
Seeing everything
Seeing that I am scared
Seeing that I hurry to get into the sunlight
Shadows following
Following me
Dancing up the walls
Chasing me across the ceiling
Never leaving . . .
Shadows.

Fun With Fluency

Underline the words that you emphasize when you read the poem aloud.

FLUENCY SPOTLIGHT

Phrasing, Rate, and Intonation

MEANING FIRST

Before the modeled reading, read aloud and discuss the passage. Pose this or another comprehension question: *What message about spiders is the author trying to pass on to the reader?* Now continue with the lesson and read the text again with a focus on fluency.

MODEL AND DISCUSS FLUENCY

Proceed with a modeled reading of "Spider" that is smooth and expressive. Use the script provided here as a sample for your own instructional dialogue with students.

> **Phrasing:** *"When we speak, we naturally clump words together in a sentence. Listen as I group certain words in this sentence: They are afraid / that spiders will / jump up / and bite them. Do you hear how jump up and bite them naturally go together? Listen to how awkward the sentence sounds when I pause after every word: They / are / afraid / that / spiders / will / jump / up / and / bite / them. Now look at this sentence where the author uses punctuation called a dash to tell the reader where to pause and which words to clump together."* (Point to and read the second sentence of the second paragraph, emphasizing the pause at each dash.)
>
> **Rate:** *"Notice that I read this passage at a natural speed—not particularly fast or slow. I read as if I were talking to all of you about spiders."*
>
> **Intonation:** *"When we speak, and also when we read fluently, we naturally emphasize certain words. For example, listen to the word I emphasize in this sentence: Many people think spiders are <u>horrible</u> creatures. I put more stress on the word horrible to add drama to the sentence and because the word horrible sounds more horrible when stretched out and spoken in such a way. When we emphasize certain words, we help communicate the author's intended meaning and make Read-Alouds more interesting to listen to."*

ALL TOGETHER NOW

Do a choral reading of "Spiders," pointing to each word as you read. Explain that this reading passage has very little punctuation to tell the reader which words to clump together, which words to emphasize, or how fast or slow to read. It is up to the reader to think about what they are reading and decide how it would sound the most natural, as if the author were in the room speaking the words.

Practice, Practice, Practice!

Partner Reading: Have partners take turns reading "Spiders." For partners of the same ability, have one student read the passage three times to a partner and receive feedback. Then have the partners switch roles. For partners of different abilities, pair above-level readers with on-level readers and on-level readers with below-level readers. The fluent reader can be a peer or an older student. First, the stronger reader models fluent reading with a paragraph or the entire passage. As the less fluent reader reads the same text aloud, the fluent reader provides assistance when needed, as well as feedback and encouragement. The less fluent reader rereads the text until it is read accurately and with fluency.

Name: _____   Date: _____

Spider

(from *Animals Nobody Loves* by Seymour Simon)

Many people think spiders are horrible creatures. They are afraid that spiders will jump up and bite them. Some people run away when they see a spider. Others try to kill any spider they see.

But spiders do not normally bite human beings. Spiders usually trap insects they prey upon—from flies and mosquitoes to grasshoppers and crickets—in beautiful silken webs. Then they bite the insect and inject a poison to quiet it down so that they can eat it. So we should remember that spiders do us a lot of good by getting rid of insect pests.

Of course, if you trap a spider and try to grab it, it may bite you. The bite of most spiders is harmless. But a few spiders, such as the black widow, can make people sick or even kill them. It's a good idea just to watch spiders and not bother them.

Fun With Fluency

You'll need a partner for this activity.

Have one partner read the first paragraph very quickly.

✳ Did the reading sound natural?   Yes   No

✳ Explain your answer. _____

_____

Now the other partner reads the second paragraph very slowly.

✳ Did the reading sound natural?   Yes   No

✳ Explain your answer. _____

_____

Together, read the third paragraph as if you were talking to someone.

✳ How did this reading sound compared to the reading of the first two paragraphs?

_____

_____

PART 2

The Power of Punctuation
An Introduction

The reading passages in Part 2 were selected to highlight the role punctuation plays in phrasing, rate, and intonation. Begin with a brief overview of punctuation marks and typographical signals and what they mean. Use the Punctuation and Signals Poster on page 22, or create your own larger version and have students fill in the chart. Students can also add to the chart as they encounter new signals.

Use the sentences below (or your own sentences) to demonstrate how punctuation and typographical signals affect meaning and provide clues for how to read text. Write the sentences on a chart.

> I love spaghetti and meatballs.
>
> I love spaghetti and meatballs!
>
> I love spaghetti and meatballs?
>
> I love spaghetti and MEATBALLS!
>
> I <u>love</u> spaghetti and meatballs.
>
> **I** love spaghetti and meatballs.
>
> I love spaghetti (and meatballs)!

After you read each sentence, talk about how the signals affected how you read them. How did the meaning of the sentence change? Can students tell you how you should read a sentence you point to *before* you read it? Have volunteers take turns reading the sentences and explaining why they read the sentence as they did. Explain that paying attention to these signals not only makes a story more interesting, it also makes the story easier to understand because, as they now see, the signals help the reader interpret the author's words and their meaning.

Punctuation and Signals Poster

Punctuation and Signals	What do you do when you see it?	Example
,	Pause at a **comma**.	Kevin collects stamps, baseball cards, and comic books.
.	Pause a bit longer at a **period**.	Bats and elephants are mammals. Owls and geese are birds.
?	Raise your voice at the end of a sentence with a **question mark** to show you are asking a question or expressing doubt.	What is your favorite food? You stayed up all night?
!	Read a sentence ending in an **exclamation point** with strong feelings of joy, fear, anger, horror, or surprise.	She's coming! Hide before we ruin the surprise! I made five baskets in a row! Help! My foot is stuck!
" "	Read the words in **quotation marks** as you think the character or speaker might say them. Sometimes quotation marks are around individual words for emphasis.	"Don't dillydally all day," said the old woman. A "green" person is someone who loves nature.
. . .	Pause a bit longer at an **ellipsis**.	"I . . . I can't believe . . . Did I really win?" asked the girl.
——	Pause a bit longer at a **dash**.	This heat—108 degrees—is unbearable.
( )	Pause before and after a **parenthesis**.	The Wagner Playground (also known as the tire-swing playground) is on East Street.
Words written in special ways: *italics* **boldface** <u>underline</u> ALL CAPS	Stress these words.	"You ate *that*?" gasped Joe. "**Ooouch!** I've been stung by a bee!" shrieked Sue. "The ball goes <u>in</u> the hoop, not <u>over</u> it," sneered Rick. "HIP, HIP, HOORAY!" shouted the team.

FLUENCY SPOTLIGHT

Commas

MEANING FIRST

Before the modeled reading, read aloud and discuss the passage. Pose these or other comprehension questions: *Where and when might this story take place? What are the clues in the text that led you to your answer?* Talk about the vocabulary in the text (*dread, courted, prospects, doused*). Now continue with the lesson and read the text again with a focus on fluency.

MODEL AND DISCUSS FLUENCY

Proceed with a modeled reading of the excerpt from *Clem's Chances*, stressing the pause at each comma. Use the script provided here as a sample for your own instructional dialogue with students.

> "Commas signal the reader to take a brief pause. Sometimes commas separate a list of items, characteristics, or events, such as in this sentence: **All in a single day I'd courted death, seen disaster, heard of massacres.** Did you hear the way I paused slightly after each event? Now look at the commas in the next sentence and listen as I pause at each: **I had a fleeting thought of turning back, but where could I go, friendless and poor and without prospects?** Listen as I read this sentence again without the commas. [Read it without pauses.] The sentence sounds choppy and unnatural—not at all like I would say it if I were speaking. The last sentence is a super-long sentence, with a whopping five commas to separate each idea. The commas are really needed here to help with the flow of the sentence: **I must have slept, for the next thing I knew, there was Hank standing over me, and I lay in a puddle of water, for a sudden rain had doused me, and even my socks were soaking wet.** The pauses also slow me down so I can visualize the many events and details in the sentence."

ALL TOGETHER NOW

Do a line-by-line echo reading of the text, stressing the commas. Point to each word on the transparency as the students follow along. After several readings, invite volunteers to read a sentence to the class in a fluent manner.

Practice, Practice, Practice!

Partner Reading: Have partners take turns reading the excerpt from *Clem's Chances*. For partners of the same ability, have one student read the passage three times to a partner and receive feedback. Then have the partners switch roles. For partners of different abilities, pair above-level readers with on-level readers and on-level readers with below-level readers. The fluent reader can be a peer or an older student. First, the stronger reader models fluent reading with a paragraph or the entire passage. As the less fluent reader reads the same text aloud, the fluent reader provides assistance when needed, as well as feedback and encouragement. The less fluent reader rereads the text until it is read accurately and with fluency.

Name: _____   Date: _____

Excerpt from Clem's Chances

by Sonia Levitin

My companions were soon worn out from the talk. I began to hear their snores. But I sat up half the night, shivering, haunted by feelings of dread. My journey had just begun. All in a single day I'd courted death, seen disaster, heard of massacres. I had a fleeting thought of turning back, but where could I go, friendless and poor and without prospects?

I must have slept, for the next thing I knew, there was Hank standing over me, and I lay in a puddle of water, for a sudden rain had doused me, and even my socks were soaking wet.

Fun With Fluency

1. Write your own sentence in which commas are used to separate a series of items, characteristics, or events, like in this sentence from the text: *All in a single day I'd courted death, seen disaster, heard of massacres.*

   _____

   _____

   _____

2. Write your own sentence in which commas are used to join two independent clauses, like in this sentence from the text: *I had a fleeting thought of turning back, but where could I go, friendless and poor and without prospects?*

   _____

   _____

   _____

FLUENCY SPOTLIGHT

Exclamation Points

MEANING FIRST

Before the modeled reading, read aloud and discuss the poem. Pose this or another comprehension question: *What might some other rules be that would fit well in this poem?* Now continue with the lesson and read the poem again with a focus on fluency.

MODEL AND DISCUSS FLUENCY

Proceed with a modeled reading of "My Mother Says I'm Sickening" stressing the sternness in your voice when you read each exclamation. Use the script provided here as a sample for your own instructional dialogue with students.

"Exclamation points let the reader know that the sentence should be read with strong feelings of excitement, joy, fear, anger, horror, determination, or surprise. Listen as I read this list of the mother's rules, which the poet has punctuated with exclamation points. [Read each exclamation sternly and with determination.] Which feeling do the exclamation points highlight? Notice that the poet also used bold type and all capital letters to write these rules. These are additional clues that tell the reader to read these sentences with lots of energy and feeling. We'll talk more about typographical signals like bold type and capital letters later."

ALL TOGETHER NOW

Begin with an echo reading of the poem, pointing to each word as the class follows along. Be sure to escalate your tone and energy when you read the list of rules. When the class is ready, lead them in a choral reading of the poem, or have a student lead the reading. When students are sufficiently familiar with the poem, have them act out the lines as they say them for added drama.

Practice, Practice, Practice!

Poetry Reading: After you model fluency with "My Mother Says I'm Sickening," have students practice reading the poem with the same phrasing, rate, and intonation you have used. Then assign a time over the next week for each student to read the poem to the class. For example, three students could read the poem during the morning meeting, two after lunch, and three at the close of the day.

Name: _____   Date: _____

My Mother Says I'm Sickening

(from *The New Kid on the Block* by Jack Prelutsky)

My mother says I'm sickening,
my mother says I'm crude,
she says this when she sees me
playing Ping-Pong with my food,
she doesn't seem to like it
when I slurp my bowl of stew,
and now she's got a list of things
she says I mustn't do—

DO NOT CATAPULT THE CARROTS!
DO NOT JUGGLE GOBS OF FAT!
DO NOT DROP THE MASHED POTATOES
ON THE GERBIL OR THE CAT!
NEVER PUNCH THE PUMPKIN PUDDING!
NEVER TUNNEL THROUGH THE BREAD!
PUT NO PEAS INTO YOUR POCKET!
PLACE NO NOODLES ON YOUR HEAD!
DO NOT SQUEEZE THE STEAMED ZUCCHINI!
DO NOT MAKE THE MELON OOZE!
NEVER STUFF VANILLA YOGURT
IN YOUR LITTLE SISTER'S SHOES!
DRAW NO FACES IN THE KETCHUP!
MAKE NO LITTLE GRAVY POOLS!

I wish my mother wouldn't make
So many useless rules.

Fun With Fluency

Read aloud the lines below. Describe what is different about the way sentence #1
sounds when read aloud with the way sentence #2 sounds when read aloud.

1. Do not juggle gobs of fat.   **2.** Do not juggle gobs of fat!

_____

_____

FLUENCY SPOTLIGHT

Question Marks

MEANING FIRST

Before the modeled reading, read aloud and discuss the passage. Pose these or other comprehension questions: *Why did Jim Davenport say he lived in extraordinary times? How did he plan to become famous?* Now continue with the lesson and read the text again with a focus on fluency.

MODEL AND DISCUSS FLUENCY

Proceed with a modeled reading of the excerpt from *The British Are Coming!*, emphasizing the rise in your voice after each question. Use the script provided here as a sample for your own instructional dialogue with students.

"When we ask a question, our voices naturally go up at the end of the question, like this: **Do you have any more comic books left?** *It is important to let your voice rise at the end of questions when you read aloud, as well. This signal helps the listener realize that a question is being asked, and it makes the reading sound natural and the way the author intended the words to sound when read aloud. Let's listen to the unique sound of questions and compare them to the sound of statements. I'm going to read this journal entry from the book* **The British Are Coming!** *without letting you see the text on the overhead. I want you to raise your hand each time you hear me read a question. [Read text aloud, noting when students raise their hands.] What did you notice about the way questions are read compared to the way statements are read?"*

ALL TOGETHER NOW

Do a choral reading of the text. Point to the words on the transparency as you read and stress the lift in your voice after each question.

Practice, Practice, Practice!

Tape-Assisted Reading: Invite students to listen to the way their voice rises when they read a question by having them make a tape of their reading of the text. Students should practice reading the text and achieve fluency before taping the text. For additional reinforcement, play select tapes of fluent reading back to the class. Is it clear each time the reader reads a question?

Name: _____   Date: _____

Excerpt from The British Are Coming!
by C. White

I'm Jim Davenport. Together we're going to become famous. You may wonder how an ordinary boy like me is going to become famous. Well, I may be ordinary, but guess what? I'm living in extraordinary times.

It's 1775. King George of England is trying to control the way the colonists (that's us) live. First he taxed practically everything we use. Then he set troops all over Boston.

The patriots (that's another name for colonists) are getting fed up. Why should we pay taxes and obey the king's soldiers? We don't even get a vote in Parliament. Something big is going to happen soon. I can just feel it.

So how's that going to make me famous? With all of this stuff going on, all I have to do is write it down in you, my trusty journal. Then I'm going to put it out there for everyone to read. My title? *The Thrilling Life of James Davenport—Boy Hero.* Now all I need is for something to happen.

Fun With Fluency

On the back of this page, write a brief journal entry using yourself or a fictional character as the subject. Like Jim Davenport, include questions throughout your journal entry. When you have finished, practice reading your journal entry. Then read your journal to a partner with fluency and expression.

FLUENCY SPOTLIGHT

Quotation Marks

MEANING FIRST

Before the modeled reading, read aloud and discuss the poem. Pose this or another comprehension question: *What feelings does the girl seem to be experiencing in this poem?* Now continue with the lesson and read the poem again with a focus on fluency.

MODEL AND DISCUSS FLUENCY

Proceed with a modeled reading of "My Dad," emphasizing the distinct voices of the father and daughter. Use the script provided here as a sample for your own instructional dialogue with students.

> "'My Dad' is a fun poem to read because it is like reading a conversation between a girl and her father. Notice the quotation marks throughout the poem. Quotation marks let us know when a person or character speaks. The quotation marks go around the actual words that are spoken—or the quote. As I read the poem, listen to the way I give each character his or her own voice. I read the dad's quotes the way I think the dad would say those words, and I do the same for the girl's quotes. To do this, I need to think about what is happening in the poem and how the characters might be feeling."

ALL TOGETHER NOW

Begin with a choral reading of "My Dad," emphasizing the two voices in the poem. When the class has reached fluency, read the poem again, with you reading the role of the dad and the class reading the quotes and narration of the girl. Did they capture the voice of the girl?

Practice, Practice, Practice!

Partner Reading: Have partners take turns reading "My Dad." For partners of the same ability, have one student read the poem three times to a partner and receive feedback. Then have the partners switch roles. For partners of different abilities, pair above-level readers with on-level readers and on-level readers with below-level readers. The fluent reader can be a peer or an older student. First, the stronger reader models fluent reading of the poem. As the less fluent reader reads the poem aloud, the fluent reader provides assistance when needed, as well as feedback and encouragement. The less fluent reader rereads the poem until it is read accurately and with fluency. After students practice making the voice of the dad and the daughter distinct, have the students read the poem together, taking the part of either the dad or the daughter.

Name: _____   Date: _____

My Dad

(by Sherri Tysinger from *Kids' Poems: Teaching Third & Fourth Graders to Love Writing Poetry*)

"Hi, Dad."
"Hey, girl. How was school?"
"It was O.K."
"O.K.? Well, what did you learn today?"
"Oh boy," I'm thinking.
Here he comes
with the question,
"Did anything happen?"
"Oh, Dad."
I go into my room and close the door,
hear some footsteps…
Here he comes.

Fun With Fluency

1. What kind of day did the girl seem to have at school?

_____

_____

2. Which clues from the poem helped you arrive at your answer?

_____

_____

_____

_____

3. How would you describe the girl's mood?

_____

_____

PART 3

Putting It All Together
An Introduction

In Part I of this book, students learn about phrasing, rate, and intonation with text that has very little punctuation or typographical signals. In Part II, students learn that punctuation marks serve as signals and help communicate how the author wants us to read the text. Putting It All Together, the third part in this book, includes eight reading passages and poems in which students encounter a variety of punctuation marks and typographical signals. Modeled reading of the texts reveals distinct moods, sentence structures, and rhythms. As you explore the passages, talk explicitly about clues in the text that indicate how the words should sound when read aloud. Hand out and review the Fluent Reading Checklist on page 32. Encourage students to refer to the list when they feel their oral reading lacks expression and fluency and want to be sure to accurately communicate the author's meaning.

Name: _____   Date: _____

Do You Do These Things When You Read?

☐ I think about the meaning of the words I read and how they would naturally sound when spoken.

☐ I make sure that what I am reading makes sense.

☐ I follow the rules of punctuation marks.

☐ I pay attention when words are written in an unusual way, such as all caps, boldface, italics, or words written very big or very small.

☐ When I read a rhyming poem or text, I emphasize the rhyming words.

☐ When I read dialogue, I read the words as I think the person or character would say them.

☐ I read at the same speed as I talk, not too slow and not too fast. But I read certain words quickly or slowly if it sounds more natural to read the words that way (for example, "Run! The bear is right behind you!").

FLUENCY SPOTLIGHT

Long and Short Sentences, Commas and Phrasing

MEANING FIRST

Before the modeled reading, read aloud and discuss the passage. Pose this or another comprehension question: *How does the mood of the scene gradually shift as the text unfolds?* Now continue with the lesson and read the text again with a focus on fluency.

MODEL AND DISCUSS FLUENCY

Proceed with a modeled reading of the excerpt from *The Music of the Dolphins*. Emphasize the pauses with each comma. Use the script provided here as a sample for your own instructional dialogue with students.

Long and Short Sentences: *"Authors are careful to use a variety of long and short sentences to create a pleasing rhythm to the words. Listen to the short and long sentences in this paragraph:* **Joyful with the coming day, I splash and whistle at a milky sun. The dolphins wake and whistle too. They are suddenly and fully aware. The ocean fills with their sound. Flukes slapping. Quick calls rising and falling. We slide under and over each other, racing through the morning waves, riding the misty lid of the sea.** *This last sentence sounds pleasing after the shorter sentences. You can imagine that a paragraph made up entirely of short, punchy sentences might sound choppy. Or a paragraph of all long, winding sentences might sound labored and long-winded."*

Commas and Phrasing: *"You'll notice that many of the longer sentences in this text have several commas. The commas signal us to pause at natural resting spots between clusters of words. Listen as I pause twice when I read this sentence:* **We slide under and over each other, racing through the morning waves, riding the misty lid of the sea.** *Now listen as I read the same sentence as if there were no commas:* **We slide under and over each other racing through the morning waves riding the misty lid of the sea.** *Compare the two readings. Which reading sounds more natural and fluid? Which reading makes it easier to understand what is happening in the sentence?"*

ALL TOGETHER NOW

Begin with a line-by-line echo reading of the text. Emphasize the text's phrasing and smooth rhythm. Conclude with a choral reading of the excerpt.

Practice, Practice, Practice!

Trio Reading: Divide the class into groups of three. Each group member reads one of the three paragraphs in the text while the others provide support when needed. Once all members agree that each has read his or her portion with fluency, they rotate the reading parts until each member has fluently read all three paragraphs.

Name: _____   Date: _____

Excerpt from The Music of the Dolphins

by Karen Hesse

I swim out to them on the murmuring sea. As I reach them, their circle opens to let me in, then re-forms. The dolphins rise and blow, floating, one eye open, the other shut in half sleep.

Joyful with the coming day, I splash and whistle at a milky sun. The dolphins wake and whistle too. They are suddenly and fully aware. The ocean fills with their sound. Flukes slapping. Quick calls rising and falling. We slide under and over each other, racing through the morning waves, riding the misty lid of the sea.

Three gulls sit on the soft shoulder of a swell. So quiet, I come with my dolphin cousins, up from below, and scare the bobbing birds. The gulls rise, screaming mad. We laugh and laugh, bright beads of dolphin noise, while above the birds dip and cry.

Fun With Fluency

With a partner, read the following sentences. Discuss the role commas play as you compare the sentence from the text with the accompanying sentence where commas are used incorrectly or omitted.

1a. As I reach them, their circle opens to let me in, then re-forms.
1b. As I reach them their, circle opens to let me, in then re-forms.

2a. The dolphins rise and blow, floating, one eye open, the other shut in half sleep.
2b. The dolphins rise and blow floating one eye open the other shut in half sleep.

3a. We slide under and over each other, racing through the morning waves, riding the misty lid of the sea.
3b. We slide, under and over, each other racing, through the, morning waves, riding the, misty lid, of the sea.

On the back of this page, describe the important role of the comma.

Dash, Typographical Signals

MEANING FIRST

Before the modeled reading, read aloud and discuss the passage. Pose this or another comprehension question: *What did you learn from this passage that you didn't know before?* Now continue with the lesson and read the text again with a focus on fluency.

MODEL AND DISCUSS FLUENCY

Proceed with a modeled reading of the excerpt "Armed Attack." Pay special attention to the punctuation and typographical signals. Use the script provided here as a sample for your own instructional dialogue with students.

Dash: *"Notice the three dashes in this reading passage. A dash often indicates that the author is going to provide additional information or an example. When you come to a dash in text, pause longer than you would for a comma. Listen as I read the first sentence:* **Army ants travel in huge groups—from 10,000 to several million.** *Did you hear the way I nearly came to a complete stop when I reached the dash? This pause provides a natural break before the authors elaborate on the first part of the sentence. Now look at this sentence and listen to what I do at each dash:* **They open wide their razor-sharp jaws—and ZAP!—slam them shut on the flesh.** *The exaggerated pause at each dash really adds drama and excitement to the sentence. It is as if the dashes in this sentence mimic the movement of a hungry army ant where the ant opens its mouth, waits a second, and then slams it shut on its victim."*

Typographical Signals: *"Looking at this same sentence with the two dashes, you'll notice that the authors wrote the word* **ZAP** *in all capital letters. While they could have written* **zap** *in lowercase, the decision to write* **zap** *as they did was a good one. The reader comes across* **ZAP!** *and reads the word with energy and force—the way the army ant's jaws come down on its victim."*

ALL TOGETHER NOW

Do a choral reading of the passage. As you point to the words on the transparency and the students follow along, stress the dashes and the energy behind *ZAP!*

Practice, Practice, Practice!

Tape-Assisted Reading: Students may readily understand that poetry and fiction are meant to be read with expression and rhythm but they may need to be reminded that nonfiction should be approached in the same way. Create a tape of *"Armed Attack."* You may want to have other adults or fluent readers create the tape to give students a variety of voices to listen to. First, students listen to the passage on tape, pointing to the words on their hard copy as they follow along. The students then read aloud with the tape, as they would in choral reading.

Name: _____ Date: _____

Armed Attack

(from *Flies Taste With Their Feet: Weird Facts About Insects* by Melvin and Gilda Berger)

Army ants travel in huge groups—from 10,000 to several million. The advancing hordes give off a smell like rotten meat! And their footsteps make a loud, frightening, hissing noise.

No one is safe from marching army ants. They attack even the biggest animals. Hundreds of ants swarm over every victim. They open wide their razor-sharp jaws—and ZAP!—slam them shut on the flesh. The ants hang on as they pull and tear at the animal. Sooner or later the creature dies of its wounds.

Fun With Fluency

Using the sentence below as a model, write a sentence that describes the way an animal might attack its prey. Don't forget to add drama to your sentence with dashes and capital letters.

They open wide their razor-sharp jaws—and ZAP!—slam them shut on the flesh.

_____

_____

_____

_____

FLUENCY SPOTLIGHT

Typographical Signals

MEANING FIRST

Before the modeled reading, read aloud and discuss the passage. Pose this or another comprehension question: *How would you describe the mood of this reading passage?* Now continue with the lesson and read the text again with a focus on fluency.

MODEL AND DISCUSS FLUENCY

Proceed with a modeled reading of the excerpt from *Harry Potter and the Sorcerer's Stone*, using your voice to create drama and suspense. Use the script provided here as a sample for your own instructional dialogue with students.

*"In the last reading passage, we saw how the author used all capital letters to add drama and excitement to the sentence. Here, J. K. Rowling uses all capital letters within dialogue to show that Hagrid is alarmed and is warning the others to get out of harm's way: **"Don't worry, it can't've gone far if it's this badly hurt, an' then we'll be able ter—GET BEHIND THAT TREE!"** The reader can truly sense the terror in this scene. It was clever the way the author had Hagrid see something shocking as he was speaking, so there is a contrast between his talking voice and his alarmed voice. It is the job of the reader to perform both voices when reading the text aloud."*

*"Writing words or sentences in all capitals is one way to reveal emotion in words. Another way is to italicize words. Look at this sentence and notice that the word **could** is italicized: **"Could a werewolf be killing unicorns?"** Harry asked. Now listen as I read the sentence. Did you hear the way I put more emphasis on the word **could**? Now listen as I read the sentence as if **could** were not in italics. When I read the sentence as it is printed, Harry sounds more concerned and frightened, doesn't he?"*

ALL TOGETHER NOW

Lead a choral reading of the text.

Practice, Practice, Practice!

Partner Reading: Have partners take turns reading the excerpt from *Harry Potter and the Sorcerer's Stone*. For partners of the same ability, have one student read the text to a partner and receive feedback. Then have the partners switch roles. For partners of different abilities, pair above-level readers with on-level readers and on-level readers with below-level readers. The fluent reader can be a peer or an older student. First, the stronger reader models fluent reading of the passage. As the less fluent reader reads the text aloud, the fluent reader provides assistance when needed, as well as feedback and encouragement. The less fluent reader rereads the text until it is read accurately and with fluency.

Name: _____   Date: _____

Excerpt from Harry Potter and the Sorcerer's Stone

by J. K. Rowling

The forest was black and silent. A little way into it they reached a fork in the earth path, and Harry, Hermione, and Hagrid took the left path while Malfoy, Neville, and Fang took the right.

They walked in silence, their eyes on the ground. Every now and then a ray of moonlight through the branches above lit a spot of silver-blue blood on the fallen leaves.

Harry saw that Hagrid looked very worried.

"*Could* a werewolf be killing the unicorns?" Harry asked.

"Not fast enough," said Hagrid. "It's not easy ter catch a unicorn, they're powerful magic creatures. I never knew one ter be hurt before."

They walked past a mossy tree stump. Harry could hear running water; there must be a stream somewhere close by. There were still spots of unicorn blood here and there along the winding path.

"You all right, Hermione?" Hagrid whispered. "Don't worry, it can't've gone far if it's this badly hurt, an' then we'll be able ter—GET BEHIND THAT TREE!"

Fun With Fluency

How might you rewrite the sentences below to make them more interesting to read? Hint: How did it sound when you hit the floor, or how did you sound when you cried out in pain?

I was walking down the hall when all of a sudden I tripped on my shoelace and fell flat on my face! I cried out in pain.

_____

_____

_____

FLUENCY SPOTLIGHT

Voice and Punctuation Typographical Signals

MEANING FIRST

Before the modeled reading, read aloud and discuss the passage. Pose this or another comprehension question: *Based on the way this letter to Elizabeth begins, does it seem that Elizabeth was very understanding about her friend having to move? Why do you think so?* Now continue with the lesson and read the text again with a focus on fluency.

MODEL AND DISCUSS FLUENCY

Proceed with a modeled reading of the excerpt from *Longer Letter Later*. Emphasize the punctuation and typographical signals that help shape the character's voice. Use the script provided here as a sample for your own instructional dialogue with students.

"This passage is fun to read aloud because the letter is full of emotion. How do we know? For one reason, the content of the letter—the meaning of the words—tells us that this character is terribly homesick and missing her friend. Second, the authors have written certain words in a special way and used punctuation to tell us to read the words in a particular way. For example, look at the beginning of the letter: **GIVE ME A BREAK!!!!!!!!! YOU KNOW THAT I DIDN'T WANT TO MOVE...THAT I WAS KIDNAPPED BY THE CHARENTS (my CHildlike pARENTS).** You can easily imagine that if this character were saying these words to Elizabeth, she would be using a loud and emotional voice, right? The use of all capital letters and not just one but many exclamation points, demands that the reader sound the way the character must feel."

"Letters often sound very conversational—that is, the words and the structure of the sentences often sound the way the writer of the letter speaks. The frequent use of ellipses show where the character would pause if she were speaking the words versus writing the words. Remember, ellipses are a bit stronger than a comma. Listen: **The night before school began here, I was sooooooooo homesick ... Not just for my old home ... but for yours too.**"

"The author did a good job of giving clues to the character's voice. This character doesn't just say **so**, she says **sooooooooooo: I was sooooooooo homesick; Anyway, it was sooooooooooooooooo weird not starting school with you.** The way a person speaks helps us know more about the person."

ALL TOGETHER NOW

Lead a choral reading of the excerpt from *Longer Letter Later*. Then invite volunteers to lead the class in a choral reading from the front of the room.

Practice, Practice, Practice!

Tape-Assisted Reading: Have students read along to a taped reading of the text. Encourage students to embody the voice of the character as they make their own taped version of the text. The boys in your class may feel a bit awkward embracing this girl character, but challenge them to pretend they are actors performing a role.

Name: _____   Date: _____

Excerpt from P.S. Longer Letter Later
(by Paula Danziger and Ann M. Martin)

September 7

Dear Elizabeth,

GIVE ME A BREAK!!!!!!!!!!!!!!!

YOU KNOW THAT I DIDN'T WANT TO MOVE . . . THAT I WAS KIDNAPPED BY THE CHARENTS (my CHildlike pARENTS) . . . Oh, okay . . . I know that it's not kidnapping if your parents want to move and their kid has to go with them . . . I know I should be used to it by this time . . . Fourth, fifth, sixth grades . . . It was a record for staying in one place.

Anyway, it was soooooooooooooo weird not starting school with you.

The night before school began here, I was sooooooo homesick . . . Not just for my old home . . . but for yours too. I kept thinking about how the nights before fifth and sixth grade we would go to each other's houses and figure out what each of us would wear for the first day of school. I was sooooo sad. I took out my copy of the scrapbooks we made before I left and looked at the pictures Barb took of us on our first days of school . . .

Fun With Fluency

Below, write a statement that calls for special treatment of words or punctuation. See the beginning of the letter for an example.

_____

_____

_____

Now give your statement to a neighbor to read. Did he or she read the statement with the expression you intended? _____ Please explain your answer.

_____

_____

_____

FLUENCY SPOTLIGHT

Phrasing With Ellipses and Hyphens

MEANING FIRST

Before the modeled reading, read aloud and discuss the poem. Pose this or another comprehension question: *What do you think the turtle means when it says, "I don't know why I bother."?* Now continue with the lesson and read the poem again with a focus on fluency.

MODEL AND DISCUSS FLUENCY

Proceed with a modeled reading of "The Turtle," paying special attention to the ellipses and hyphens that slow down the reading rate. Use the script provided here as a sample for your own instructional dialogue with students.

Ellipses: *"'The Turtle' is a fun poem to read aloud because the poet guides us to read the poem in a very specific way. Notice all the ellipses throughout the poem. These frequent and substantial pauses make the pace of the poem sound the way the turtle moves—very slowly. Listen as I read the first sentence and note the effectiveness of each pause:* **The turtle takes . . one . . . . step . . . and . . . . then a-n-o-t-h-e-r.** *The poet is very clever with his use of ellipses and the pauses make perfect sense in this poem. In another text or poem, this punctuation would make the words sound choppy and very unnatural."*

Hyphens Within Words: *"Using hyphens within words is another trick the poet uses to show the slowness of the turtle and to slow us down as we read the poem. Let's look closely at the first sentence again. The ellipses slow us down between each word, while the hyphens in the last word slow us down as we read the last word:* **The turtle takes . . one . . . . step . . . and . . . . then a-n-o-t-h-e-r.** *What a clever way to use punctuation!"*

ALL TOGETHER NOW

Begin with choral readings of "The Turtle." Then add movement to the poem. As one side of the class reads the poem, the other side acts out each line. Then the sides switch roles. Or have individual students perform the movement in the front of the class as the class reads the poem.

Practice, Practice, Practice!

Cross-Age Reading: Include this poem in a group of poems that students will read for a younger audience. After students practice reading the poem on their own, have them read the poem to a reading partner who provides feedback. The younger students would also enjoy the added movement, either by themselves or by another student who acts out each line.

Name: _____   Date: _____

The Turtle

(by Arnold Spilka from *Monkeys Write Terrible Letters***)**

The turtle

takes . . one . . . . step

. . . and . . . . then

a-n-o-t-h-e-r.

. . . then he . . . slow-ly

. . looks . . . . around

. . . . . . and says,

"I don't . . . .

. . know . . . why . .

I . . . . . b-o-t-h-e-r."

Fun With Fluency

Below is a version of "The Turtle" without the original punctuation and line
structure. Read aloud the version below.

The turtle takes one step and then another.

Then he slowly looks around and says,

"I don't know why I bother."

Compare this version with the original. What is the same? What is different about
the way the two poems sound when read aloud?

_____

_____

_____

PART 3

Putting It All Together

FLUENCY SPOTLIGHT

Dialogue

MEANING FIRST

Before the modeled reading, read aloud and discuss the passage. Pose these or other comprehension questions: *Have you ever thought about opening a business one day? What kind of business would you open?* Now continue with the lesson and read the text again with a focus on fluency.

MODEL AND DISCUSS FLUENCY

Proceed with a modeled reading of the excerpt from *Kater Kids*, distinguishing each character's voice and tone. Use the script provided here as a sample for your own instructional dialogue with students.

Dialogue: *"How do we decide how to make characters sound when we read dialogue aloud? The best way is to think about the meaning of the words the character speaks. How do you think you would say those words if you were in the character's shoes? Or how do you think the character would say the words if they were able to speak for themselves? Sometimes, authors give us clues as to how to read a character's words. Here's an example:* **"Don't unwrap anything!"** *scolded his sister.* **"That's all the food for the party."** *Do you see a clue the author gave for how to read this sentence? The author could have written* **said his sister**, *but instead, she chose her words carefully and wrote,* **scolded his sister**. *That way, we know that Kate would say these words as a firm warning versus a gentle request."*

ALL TOGETHER NOW

Do an echo reading of the passage, one quote at a time.

Practice, Practice, Practice!

Trio Reading: In groups of three, have students read the parts of Kate, Katie, and Bobby. Students can use highlighters to color-code each character's dialogue. Once fluency is achieved, students rotate roles until they have read all three.

Name: _____   Date: _____

Excerpt from Kater Kids

by Anne Miranda

"Preheat the oven. Use 2 cups flour," mumbled Kate as she made the cake.

"Cream the butter and sugar," read her friend Katie. She was making the frosting.

Kate's brother Bobby bounced into the kitchen. "What are you up to?" he asked. "Are you making a cake?"

"Sorry. This cake is for Andy Kline," said his sister. "We're catering his birthday party tomorrow."

Bobby stuck his head into the refrigerator. He wanted something to drink. "What's all this? Looks appetizing!"

"Don't unwrap anything!" scolded his sister. "That's all the food for the party."

"Since when do you do parties?" asked Bobby.

"Since we made the food for your mother's bridge group. All her friends want us to cater their birthdays," said Katie.

"So I get the leftovers the next day. Awesome!" said Bobby, rubbing his tummy and licking his lips. "You need any help?"

"Actually, Bobby, we could use a hand. If you could help us set up and clean up tomorrow, we would really appreciate it," said Kate.

"Sure," said Bobby. "For a slice of cake."

Fun With Fluency

What is the clue word given in the second sentence of this text? _____

What kind of mood is Bobby in as he makes his entrance? _____

How do you know? _____

_____

FLUENCY SPOTLIGHT

Dialogue, Question Marks, and Intonation

MEANING FIRST

Before the modeled reading, read aloud and discuss the poem. Pose these or other comprehension questions: *Do you like this poem? Why or why not? In what ways is this poem unique?* Now continue with the lesson and read the poem again with a focus on fluency.

MODEL AND DISCUSS FLUENCY

Proceed with a modeled reading of "Talking to the Horse Trainer." Distinguish the voice of the two characters and emphasize the rise in your voice with each question. Use the script provided here as a sample for your own instructional dialogue with your students.

Dialogue: *"This is a fun poem to read! I love the way the poet essentially wrote a quirky piece of conversation between two people. As I read the words of each character, I think about what their personalities are like. Then I think about how they might say the words. I can imagine that the horse trainer is very patient in this interview, but then becomes a bit irritated with the questions toward the end. Listen as my tone changes about three quarters of the way down for the horse trainer. [Read the poem accordingly.] I could also read the horse trainer's dialogue as if he is not at all irritated with the questions and continue with the same laidback tone I used at the beginning. Listen to the way that version sounds." [Read the poem accordingly.]*

Question Marks and Intonation: *"In this poem, there are many questions asked by both characters. Not all questions sound the same, however. We know that when we ask a question or read a question, our voice rises at the end of the sentence. Listen as I read the first several questions of the poem. But sometimes, a question can sound more like a statement, depending on how you say it. For example, if I make the horse trainer sound angry, the following question can sound like a demand for a reply:* **"What's your point?"** *You didn't hear my voice rise on the word* **point***. I made the question sound more like a statement that ends in an exclamation point."*

ALL TOGETHER NOW

Do an echo reading of "Talking to the Horse Trainer," with you reading the part of the questioner and the class reading the part of the horse trainer. Then switch roles. Or divide the class in half and have each half read a character and then switch.

Practice, Practice, Practice!

Poetry Duet: Have partners continue reading, with one partner as the questioner and the other partner as the horse trainer. Partners provide feedback and support to each other and practice reading the poem as a duet until they are satisfied with their fluency. They can then perform the poem for the class.

Name: _____   Date: _____

Talking to the Horse Trainer
(by Nancy Springer from *Music of Their Hooves*)

"You been kicked?"

"Yep."

"Did it hurt?"

"Yep."

"You been bitten?"

"Yep."

"That hurt too?"

"Uh-huh."

"Been run away with?"

"Some days."

"Take a fall?"

"Now and then."

"Get stepped on?"

"Once."

"More than once."

"That's true."

"How many times?"

"Maybe twice."

"More than that."

"What's your point?"

"Look at me."

"Okay, I'm looking at you. So?"

"How come you still love horses?

"How come I still love you?"

Fun With Fluency

Write your own dialogue between a parent and a child, following the format in "Talking to a Horse Trainer." Decide on the mood you want to show, and write the dialogue in a way that will create it. Have a friend read it and see if he or she reads it with the expression you wanted.

_____

_____

_____

_____

_____

_____

_____

_____

_____

_____

_____

_____

_____

PART 3

Putting It All Together

FLUENCY SPOTLIGHT

Commas and Phrasing, Rhyme and Intonation

MEANING FIRST

Before the modeled reading, read aloud and discuss the chant. Pose this or another comprehension question: *Sometimes kids recite chants like this one as they play jump rope. Why do you think that is?* Now continue with the lesson and read the chant again with a focus on fluency.

MODEL AND DISCUSS FLUENCY

Proceed with a modeled reading of the chant, stressing the pause at each comma. Use the script provided here as a sample for your own instructional dialogue with students.

Commas and Phrasing: *"This chant, like all chants, has a definite rhythm. There are lots of commas in this chant that help create the rhythm. Commas are signals that remind the reader to take a brief pause. Notice in this chant that there is a comma in the same place on each line—in the middle of the line and at the end. As I read the chant again, I'm going to raise my hand each time I come to a comma. Listen to the way I pause each time. [With one hand, point to each word on the transparency as you read, and raise the other hand at each comma.] In addition to letting us know when to pause, the commas also serve to cluster certain words together. Let's see what happens when I put commas in different places and read the chant. [With an overhead pen, stick commas in different spots or rewrite the sentences, e.g., Ooo-ah wanna, piece, of pie, Pie too, sweet wanna piece of, meat.] What happened to our rhythm? Remember that commas have an important job. They remind the reader to pause and they group words together. As a result, they help sentences have a smooth and natural rhythm."*

Rhyme and Intonation: *"This chant is a rhyming chant, which means we have the opportunity to emphasize the rhyming words when we read the poem aloud. Stressing the rhyming words in a poem or chant gives the text an easy flow and rhythm when read out loud: Ooo-ah, wanna piece of pie, Pie too sweet, wanna piece of meat, Meat too tough, wanna ride a bus. You may have noticed that ah and pie and tough and bus are not true rhymes, but they sound similar enough to work in this chant. Which words should be emphasized in the rest of the poem?"*

ALL TOGETHER NOW

Do a choral reading of "Mighty Midgets," pointing to each word as you read from the transparency. Can students feel the sense of amazement behind the words?

ALL TOGETHER NOW

Begin with a line-by-line echo reading of the chant. Point to each word on the transparency as the students follow along. Then divide the class in half and have the two groups alternately read each line. (Have one group read the first line and the second group read the second line, etc.) Choral-read the chant in this manner several times, emphasizing the pauses and the rhythm the pauses create. Encourage students to have fun with the chant, moving their heads and bodies to the rhythm of the words.

Practice, Practice, Practice!

Cross-Age Reading: Cross-age reading creates a wonderfully authentic reason to practice and perform. Have students practice choral-reading the chant in small groups. When they have mastered the text, send each group into a class of a lower grade to perform the chant. The performance can consist of reading the chant three times, and students can encourage their audience to clap to the rhythm of the chant.

Name: _____   **Date:** _____

Untitled Chant

(from *Writing Funny Bone Poems* by Paul Janeczko)

Ooo-ah, wanna piece of pie,

Pie too sweet, wanna piece of meat,

Meat too tough, wanna ride a bus,

Bus was full, wanna ride a bull,

Bull too fat, want your money back,

Money too green, wanna jelly bean,

Jelly bean not cooked, wanna read a book,

Book not read, wanna go to bed.

So close your eyes and count to ten,

And if you miss, start all over again.

Fun With Fluency

1. Which line from the chant is your favorite? Why?

_____

_____

_____

2. How do you think this chant would sound if there were no commas? Explain your answer.

_____

_____

_____

3. Create your own line to follow the line: *Book not read, wanna go to bed.*

_____

_____

Appendix
Phrased Text Lessons

Watch / out! / That / cow / might / slime / you / with / its / long / tongue!
Do you have students whose staccato, word-by-word reading has
become a habit? These students put so much attention on decoding
the words that there is little energy left over to focus on how the
words relate to each other and the overall text. Even if the students
are reading the words accurately, their comprehension is in
jeopardy because they are not grouping the words into meaningful
phrases. It is often the phrases that hold the meaning, rather than
individual words. These students need explicit instruction in
chunking written words into meaningful segments. One way
to do this is through the Phrased Text Lesson (PTL)
(Rasinski, 1994; 2003).

PTL provides students with actual cues (slashes) embedded
in the text that signal to the reader when to pause. A single
slash at the end of a phrase break indicates a short pause,
while a double slash at the end of a sentence indicates
a longer pause: Watch out! // That cow / might slime you /
with its long tongue! // Modeling how to phrase text with
tangible cues is an effective strategy for improving students'
phrasing and overall reading (Rasinski, 1990; 1994).

On page 52 is Rasinski's (2003) step-by-step Phrased Text
Lesson. He recommends approximately hundred-word
reading passages or segments from texts that students have
recently read or will read in the near future.

Use the phrased reading passages on pages 53–55 along
with the guidelines.

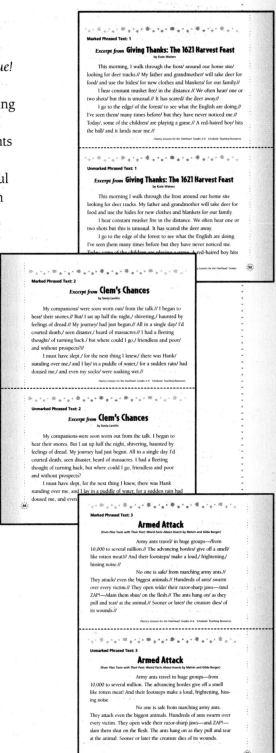

Phrased Text Lesson: A Quick Guide

The PTL is designed to be taught to individual students or small groups, over two consecutive days, 10 to 15 minutes each day.

Day 1

1. Give each student a copy of a phrase-cued text, (such as those found on pages 48 to 50.)

2. Remind students of the importance of reading in phrases, not word by word.

3. Explain the purpose of phrase markings on the text.

4. Read the text to students several times, emphasizing and slightly exaggerating the phrases.

5. Read the text with students two or three times in a choral fashion, emphasizing good phrasing and expression.

6. Have students read the text orally with a partner, two or three readings per student.

7. Have students perform the text orally for the group.

Day 2

Repeat the procedure from the first day, using the same text *without the phrase boundaries* marked to help students transfer their understanding of phrased reading to conventional text.

(Excerpted from *The Fluent Reader* by Timothy Rasinski, Scholastic, 2003)

Excerpt from Giving Thanks: The 1621 Harvest Feast
by Kate Waters

This morning I walk through the frost/ around our home site/ looking for deer tracks.// My father and grandmother/ will take deer for food/ and use the hides/ for new clothes and blankets/ for our family.//

I hear constant musket fire/ in the distance.// We often hear/ one or two shots/ but this is unusual.// It has scared/ the deer away.//

I go to the edge/ of the forest/ to see what the English are doing.// I've seen them/ many times before/ but they have never noticed me.// Today,/ some of the children/ are playing a game.// A red-haired boy/ hits the ball/ and it lands near me.//

Fluency Lessons for the Overhead: Grades 4–6 Scholastic Teaching Resources

---

Unmarked Phrased Text: 1

Excerpt from Giving Thanks: The 1621 Harvest Feast
by Kate Waters

This morning I walk through the frost around our home site looking for deer tracks. My father and grandmother will take deer for food and use the hides for new clothes and blankets for our family.

I hear constant musket fire in the distance. We often hear one or two shots but this is unusual. It has scared the deer away.

I go to the edge of the forest to see what the English are doing. I've seen them many times before but they have never noticed me. Today, some of the children are playing a game. A red-haired boy hits the ball and it lands near me.

Excerpt from Clem's Chances

by Sonia Levitin

My companions/ were soon worn out/ from the talk.// I began to hear/ their snores.// But/ I sat up half the night,/ shivering,/ haunted by feelings of dread.// My journey/ had just begun.// All in a single day/ I'd courted death,/ seen disaster,/ heard of massacres.// I had a fleeting thought/ of turning back,/ but where could I go,/ friendless and poor/ and without prospects?//

I must have slept,/ for the next thing I knew,/ there was Hank/ standing over me,/ and I lay/ in a puddle of water,/ for a sudden rain/ had doused me,/ and even my socks/ were soaking wet.//

Fluency Lessons for the Overhead: Grades 4–6 Scholastic Teaching Resources

Excerpt from Clem's Chances

by Sonia Levitin

My companions were soon worn out from the talk. I began to hear their snores. But I sat up half the night, shivering, haunted by feelings of dread. My journey had just begun. All in a single day I'd courted death, seen disaster, heard of massacres. I had a fleeting thought of turning back, but where could I go, friendless and poor and without prospects?

I must have slept, for the next thing I knew, there was Hank standing over me, and I lay in a puddle of water, for a sudden rain had doused me, and even my socks were soaking wet.

Marked Phrased Text: 3

Armed Attack

(from *Flies Taste With Their Feet: Weird Facts About Insects* by Melvin and Gilda Berger)

Army ants travel/ in huge groups—/from 10,000 to several million.// The advancing hordes/ give off a smell/ like rotten meat!// And their footsteps/ make a loud,/ frightening,/ hissing noise.//

No one is safe/ from marching army ants.// They attack/ even the biggest animals.// Hundreds of ants/ swarm over every victim.// They open wide/ their razor-sharp jaws—/and ZAP!—/slam them shut/ on the flesh.// The ants hang on/ as they pull and tear/ at the animal.// Sooner or later/ the creature dies/ of its wounds.//

Fluency Lessons for the Overhead: Grades 4–6 Scholastic Teaching Resources

Unmarked Phrased Text: 3

Armed Attack

(from *Flies Taste With Their Feet: Weird Facts About Insects* by Melvin and Gilda Berger)

Army ants travel in huge groups—from 10,000 to several million. The advancing hordes give off a smell like rotten meat! And their footsteps make a loud, frightening, hissing noise.

No one is safe from marching army ants. They attack even the biggest animals. Hundreds of ants swarm over every victim. They open wide their razor-sharp jaws—and ZAP!—slam them shut on the flesh. The ants hang on as they pull and tear at the animal. Sooner or later the creature dies of its wounds.

Bibliography

Professional

Allington, R.L. "Fluency: The Neglected Reading Goal." *The Reading Teacher*. 36 (1983): 556–561.

Nathan, R.G., & K.E. Stanovich. "The Causes and Consequences of Differences in Reading Fluency." *Theory Into Practice*. 30 (1991): 176–184

National Reading Panel. "Report of the National Reading Panel: Teaching Children to Read." Report of the Subgroups. Washington, DC: U.S. Department of Health and Human Services, National Institutes of Health, 2000.

Rasinski, T.V. "Developing Syntactic Sensitivity in Reading Through Phrase-Cued Texts." *Intervention in School and Clinic*. 29, No. 3 (January 1994).

Rasinski, T.V. *The Fluent Reader: Oral Reading Strategies for Building Word Recognition, Fluency, and Comprehension*. New York: Scholastic, 2003.

Rasinski, T.V. "The Effects of Cued Phrase Boundaries in Texts." Bloomington, IN: ERIC Clearinghouse on Reading and Communication Skills, (ED 313 689) 1990.

Snow, C. E., S. M. Burns, & P. Griffin, (Eds.). *Preventing Reading Difficulties in Young Children*. Washington, DC: National Academy Press, 1998.

Wolf, M., & Katzir-Cohen, T. "Reading Fluency and Its Intervention." *Scientific Studies of Reading*. 5 (2001): 211–238.

Reading Passages

Giving Thanks: The 1621 Harvest Feast by Kate Waters (Scholastic, 2001)

"Shadows" by Anna Hutt from *Kids' Poems: Teaching Third & Fourth Graders to Love Writing Poetry* by Regie Routman (Scholastic, 2000)

"Spider" from *Animals Nobody Loves* by Seymour Simon (Chronicle Books, 2001)

Clem's Chances by Sonia Levitin (Scholastic, Apple Paperbacks, 2001)

"My Mother Says I'm Sickening" by Jack Prelutsky from *The New Kid on the Block* by Jack Prelutsky (HarperCollins, 1984)

The British Are Coming! by C. White (Scholastic)

"My Dad" by Sherri Tysinger from *Kids' Poems: Teaching Third & Fourth Graders to Love Writing Poetry* by Regie Routman (Scholastic, 2000)

The Music of the Dolphins by Karen Hesse (Scholastic, 1996)

"Armed Attack" from *Flies Taste With Their Feet: Weird Facts About Insects* by Melvin and Gilda Berger (Scholastic, 1997)

Harry Potter and the Sorcerer's Stone by J. K. Rowling (Scholastic, 1997)

P.S. Longer Letter Later by Paula Danziger and Ann M. Martin (Scholastic, 1998)

"The Turtle" by Arnold Spilka from *Monkeys Write Terrible Letters* by Arnold Spilka (Wordsong/Boyds Mill Press, 1994)

Kater Kids by Anne Miranda (Scholastic, 2002)

"Talking to the Horse Trainer" by Nancy Springer from *Music of Their Hooves* by Nancy Springer (Wordsong/Boyds Mill Press, 1994)

"Untitled Chant" from *Writing Funny Bone Poems* by Paul Janeczko (Wordsong/Boyds Mill Press, 1994)